POEMS OF THE SPIRIT

Martha Woodruff-Duncan

ISBN 978-1-63874-536-5 (paperback)
ISBN 978-1-63903-689-9 (hardcover)
ISBN 978-1-63874-537-2 (digital)

Copyright © 2022 by Martha Woodruff-Duncan

All rights reserved. No part of this publication may be reproduced, distributed, or transmitted in any form or by any means, including photocopying, recording, or other electronic or mechanical methods without the prior written permission of the publisher. For permission requests, solicit the publisher via the address below.

Christian Faith Publishing
832 Park Avenue
Meadville, PA 16335
www.christianfaithpublishing.com

Printed in the United States of America

I dedicate this book of poems, *Poems of the Spirit*, to my late husband, Andrew David Duncan. Honestly, without giving Andrew eighteen of the last years of my life, in this lifetime, this book of poems would have never been written. Andrew being an artist and a sculptor, a designer, an illustrator, he was contemplative in his nature, a profound thinker, demonstrating this briefly throughout our relationship. He spoke such words as: "We all have too much false pride," as he went down the hall in our home into his office area. He had no reason whatsoever to express these words in those moments of now. Neither of us were discussing anything. I was busy in the kitchen area. On another occasion, when I was talking to him about something that upset me, he looked at me out of the corner of his left eye and said, "Look for the silver lining in every situation." Reaching an understanding, an awareness—spiritually speaking—these are profound words.

I commenced writing *Poems of the Spirit* after Andrew passed. When the words in my poems began to rhyme, I felt deeply that Andrew was sending me those words. As I read back the words to each poem in my draft notes, the title of the poem would come to me. This, too, I felt Andrew sent to me from spirit. In my thoughts and in my prayers, I would thank him if he was helping me write each poem.

Acknowledgments

I acknowledge the authors of the wonderful books of enlightenment that I have read, instilling me with the wisdom, understanding, and awareness—spiritually speaking—to write *Poems of the Spirit*: The late Ruth Montgomery, passing in 2000, *A World Beyond;* Eckhart Tolle, *The Power of Now;* Neale Donald Walsch, *Conversations with God:* An Uncommon Dialogue, trilogy of three. These books came into my life when I was ready to receive their message of spiritual enlightenment.

Without these authors and their spiritual message of enlightenment, *Poems of the Spirit* would have never been written.

Journey of Life

◇◇

We live a life through choice with strength and grace, even though we feel misplaced. We journey through, and when we view, we see that life is something we need to do.

Original poem by Martha Woodruff-Duncan Copyright

THE BAND OF LIFE

Face life with a smile because in a while, everything may turn wild. Nothing remains the same, and there is no one to blame, except ourselves with our thoughts and our feelings.

We perpetuate a situation by hanging on to it, by feeling bad, by being mad. Be glad; don't be sad. Take what steps you can, let yourself expand, lend a helping hand, feel grand, and allow the band of your life to play on. It will soon be gone, way beyond, and we move on. On to here, on to there, on to everywhere. And through all of our woes, God always knows that we are doing the best that we can.

Feel what we feel and allow it to peel away. Away from our thoughts where it just rots.

This journey of life that can turn into a maze is full of grace. When we understand that we choose it in advance for feelings—

CONTINUATION...

what it feels like to go through this and go through that—we no longer fight, feel spite, but live in our bright light.

Original poem by Martha Woodruff-Duncan Copyright

We Make Mistakes

◇◇◇

For heaven's sake, we make mistakes. We feel so blue, what shall we do? This is just a moment in time, soon we shall feel sublime. We yearn for more of all that is because we develop from its abyss. Why fall and crawl when we can stand tall with strength and grace, looking at life straight in the face. Pick it up, I say. Go out and play, have fun along the way, but for heaven's sake make room for wisdom's way, it shall never lead you astray

Original poem by Martha Woodruff-Duncan Copyright

Fall from Grace

To fall from grace, flat on our face, is such a sad place. It hurts so much to try to touch the depth of our soul, which is as bold as it is old. We weep so deep as we feel the steep climb back up. Back up to where? Back up to what? Turn around, face your dismay, and allow the play of your life to unfold. Be bold, find the gold, it is there within the depth of your soul.

Original poem by Martha Woodruff-Duncan Copyright

The Egoic Mind

The egoic mind is never kind, it keeps us blind. It is always there playing its games of unfair. The egoic mind never strays far away, it hangs around to make us frown. Do we dare challenge the egoic mind at its games of unfair and say, "I don't care"? No! We play along, we sing its song, we never allow it to be gone. It destroys our Being and everything.

How great it is to sing a new song, witness a new dawn, and allow the egoic mind to be gone. Be friends with what is and live in bliss. Soon you will feel the kiss of love and witness a white dove flying high up above, even if just in our mind. Let us be kind to ourselves, to others, and see what happens?... Like a little child playing wild we become mild, and the egoic mind begins to disappear into the sphere where there is no fear—the realm of highly evolved souls. We shed a tear of gladness, no more sadness, and we feel our state of Being. Forgive, forget, let it go, choose peace.

Original poem by Martha Woodruff-Duncan Copyright

The Cosmic Wheel

When our days are done, our moments of now have spun, and we've had our fun, there is nothing else to do but sit and coo like the pigeons do as we review. And review we will, as we let it all spill. If we start to feel ill, as we let it all spill, it's time to sit and coo like the pigeons do.

What we sow, we reap, this is important to know. It is also important to know that when we reap what we have sowed, our soul needs it, our soul wants it. This is why we sow to create the circumstances or situation necessary for our soul to go through the experience of reaping what we have sowed. But when we forgive, let go of spite, we see the light. We allow it to be, we go free. When we understand this, we no longer experience regret, we just forget. It is as it is.

The Cosmic Wheel, where none of it is real—just what we feel—is all we need to know, and allow the rest to flow where it needs to go.

Original poem by Martha Woodruff-Duncan Copyright

TO GROW OLD

◇◇

I have grown old, but I walk bold wearing the gold that my soul has gained from the experiences it has chosen to venture into in this lifetime. I feel sublime to know that all the time that I live in this lifetime my soul will gain more gold, I will walk bolder as I get older, and at the end, I will let it all go, let it all flow into the river of forever where there is no never, there is just now.

Original poem by Martha Woodruff-Duncan Copyright

Feelings

We choose it in advance, we dance off our pants, and when it's time to glance we see that we have danced and pranced for feelings—what it feels like. We must put it down and not sit and frown. It's much, much better to feel like a clown and not let ourselves down, knowing that we have done it all for feelings.

I can't say it enough, that all of this stuff that we go through is for feelings. We fill up our urn, but continue to yearn for more of this and that, get big and fat like a lazy cat on feelings. We can't let it go, we can't let it flow, and just sit and know that we've done it all for feelings. It's time to move on, let it all be gone, and be who we are—lights of Being, knowing and love, as created in the beginning in Its image and likeness—back home to our fifth-dimensional consciousness. No more to swear, knowing that it's all fair, and as we begin to pair with those who have gone where we have gone—highly evolved souls—we let it all melt like ice as we take off our disguise and see with clear eyes.

CONTINUATION...

When we learn to let go—embrace all of our experiences for what they are—feelings, we start to grow, glow, move forward into a higher level of awareness; we go back home to who we really are. How great it is to feel this bliss, the bliss of knowing who we really are. It feels so good to be kind and pay it no mind to this or that, knowing that it's all arranged so there is nothing so strange as we feel the pain of gain. No more to be tangled up in our chosen life experiences in physical form. No more to be stuck in the mud, chewing our cud. We meet our fate, we clean our slate, and we move on, let it all be gone. What we cause another to feel, we shall feel it too. What we cause another to experience, we shall experience it too. Karmic debt is always met. This is a Universal Law. When we understand this, when we know this, we stop jamming up the works and let it go, let it flow.

Blessed are those who forgive their foes who have stepped on their toes, for they know who they are, and because of that they go afar.

It is as it is for everyone who can call it a bluff and shake it all off with a fluff, like a wise old owl. We go afar knowing who we are.

Original poem by Martha Woodruff-Duncan Copyright

Mundane

My day is done, I've sung my song, and all that's left is what's going on. There will be a new dawn, making room for a new song. But is any of it real? No. Just what we feel. The feelings that we gain is all that remains, everything else is just mundane. But without mundane there is no gain, we remain plain. It's okay to remain plain, because one day we shall experience mundane, just for the feelings that we gain, if we so choose.

Original poem by Martha Woodruff-Duncan Copyright

Connecting and Interacting with the Elements of our Planet Earth

When we allow ourselves to connect and interact with the elements of our Planet Earth, the elements all around us—the birds, the bees, the rocks, the trees, the whispering insects in Summer's breeze, which life-forms are vibrating at different frequencies than our human species' physical form—we are connecting with all that is. When we allow ourselves to feel this connection, to interact with it, we move into a state of Being as all those life-forms already exist in. We blend with them, we move with them, we feel their life-form energy. We move into a state of awareness with all that is.

Hug a tree, speak to the bumblebee as it goes flying by so high. Let yourself be free with the birds in the trees. But don't try to catch a bumblebee because it will fight you, bite you. Bumblebees, by

CONTINUATION...

nature, are born to be free, and so are we wrapped in our human species' physical form.

The elements that fly so high as they say, "Hi and bye," are defensive by nature.

The beautiful roses with thorns that scorn are defensive in their nature. They have to be treated with care when they feel we are being unfair—cutting their stems down to bring them into our homes, placing them in vases with water to adorn our homes with their lovely beauty and fragrance.

The new rose being cultivated now is without thorns. I have noticed that this new rose without thorns has no fragrance at all. But this does not mean that it is not a beautiful rose. It is a rose that has been genetically altered in its cultivation, but beautiful it is, indeed.

I have also noticed that roses that grow in our domestic gardens all have thorns that scorn when being handled without consideration. These are the most beautiful of all the roses because of their lovely fragrance, nothing has been taken away from their original cultivation.

Some other bushes that sprout lovely flowers with lovely fragrances—the honeysuckle, the lilac—remain the same—unaltered because they cause no harm. They do not fight or bite when their stems are being cut down, they just are. They, too, are brought into

CONTINUATION...

our homes to be placed in vases with water for adornment because of their beauty and lovely fragrance.

When all is done, their moments of now have spun, they too will be disposed of in a dignified manner—placed in bins for recycle where they will be taken to be processed and transformed into yet another form of life—fertilizer for the growth of new roses, new flower bushes of lovely fragrances. When their remains of what was lovely are not disposed of in an appropriate, dignified manner—recycled, but dumped into the household trash—this, too, will be accounted for.

It goes on and on this recycling, this transforming into yet another form of life, leaving Planet Earth, the Emerald of our Universe, a lovely place where we can feel, touch, smell, experience, and be. Be one with it, feel it deeply, respect it. Allow it to be with glee. Let us go free like the bumblebee.

Until and unless we move into this state of connection, this state of Being with all that is, we are not yet achieving oneness with God, we are not advancing beyond the mind of man.

I am the sun, I am the moon, I am the stars that fill our night sky so high, I am the rain, I am the snow that falls to cover all, I am the wind. I Am. We are all part of the Godhead, our Divine Father, the Creator of us all and our Divine Universe. There is no separation,

CONTINUATION...

there is no division. We are all part of God's Divine Plan. To feel otherwise is arrogant and ignorant.

Original poem by Martha Woodruff-Duncan Copyright

To Live in the Past

To live in the past where everything lasts—perpetuates—is to not let it go, to not let it flow into the river of forever where there is no never.

When we take off the disguise, we see with clear eyes, and we no longer need to surmise. In a little while we start to smile. We accept what is and embrace the bliss of each moment of now.

When I look back at my life now—this stuttering, sputtering, nincompoop as I knew and saw myself—I cry, but not tears of sadness but tears of gladness. Gladness for my sadness, for allowing it to be, and then letting it go free. Gladness for feeling it deeply—what it felt like.

When I stopped struggling, when I stopped resisting my stuttering, sputtering self, the stuttering stopped. A fresh wind blew in, and the turbulence within me stopped. I flopped inside, allowing the peace of Being to set me free.

CONTINUATION...

From that moment forward I spoke calmly, peacefully, acknowledging my new self, allowing myself to be, and feeling the glee of the calm wind within me and all about me.

How good it felt not to have to feel the pain of fear, the pain of smear from those who jeered, the pain of where can I hide to abide from the pain of who I am and what I am, and have no one to blame because I came here on my own, it was my choice alone. I did so to know, to grow—for feelings—what it feels like. We cannot walk in another person's shoes until we have walked in those shoes.

Original poem by Martha Woodruff-Duncan Copyright

To Forgive

◇◇

When we forgive, when we forget, when we let it go, let it flow, we choose peace, we live in ease, we feel the breeze like a soft rain. As we review without refrain, we see that we have no one to blame. We see and feel the gain inside each blame. We move into a state of awareness—our state of Being—where we are free and see that there is nothing else to be.

Original poem by Martha Woodruff-Duncan Copyright

To Pretend

To pretend to be glad when we really feel sad is very bad. This makes us mad, and even more sad, and we become hard like wood.

To pretend to be is to not live in glee, is to not be free. We go about to and fro, pretending though. We do not feel sublime, what a waste of time.

We feel split; we throw a fit because nothing fits. But in reality, everything fits like two snug mitts.

To pretend is okay, but we have to actually feel that way—acknowledge that we are pretending. Don't squeal, just feel, and allow yourself to heal. Go within, go without; just please don't shout, live in doubt, causing you to pout. Be friends with the present moment of now. Embrace what is, don't hiss, and live in bliss.

Original poem by Martha Woodruff-Duncan Copyright

A Poem for Children

Children are nice, sugar and spice. They hate being kissed, but they love being missed. They are full of this, they are full of that, and through it all, they just love having a ball. They play like this, they play like that, do this, do that, be a brat.

Children will grin as they let it all spin because they know they can always win.

A child is born without scorn, but they soon discover what it is to mourn. They lose a cat, they lose a dog, they lose a frog, they feel it deeply—what it feels like. But they let it go, they let it flow because they know that it has to be, so they set it free.

Children don't care either way as long as they can stay and play and have a lot of fun. Fun is their thing; being loved is their dream. Children must be loved, children must be understood, and not made to feel hard like wood.

They tease, they taunt, they jeer, and because of that, they fear. They know whomever they smear, they will be smeared too. They

CONTINUATION...

know the Law as it applies, and because of that, they have no lies. Children are very wise.

Original poem by Martha Woodruff-Duncan Copyright

Summer's Trees

Summer's trees, like canopies, they bow their emerald-green branches with such great ease and speak to us in Summer's breeze. Too busy we are to open our eyes and discover their disguise. But one day, not far away, we shall all open our eyes to see our graceful trees as they bow their emerald-green branches like canopies and speak to us in Summer's breeze.

Original poem by Martha Woodruff-Duncan Copyright

Spring

The sounds and sights and smells of Spring have such a ring, they bring us joy in everything: the sound of a nighthawk squawk on an early Spring night; the sight of emerald-green leaves as they bud from the branches of their trees; the smell of honeysuckle, lilac, and the many variety of wildflowers that surround us in their fragrance of joy. Joy of life, joy of Being, joy of everything.

Original poem by Martha Woodruff-Duncan Copyright

Summer

Summer is gone, but not for long; it shall return with its sweet song: the sounds of birds and bees, the whispering of insects in Summer's breeze, the rustling of emerald-green leaves in Summer's trees. Just as we in physical form have transformation too—life and death and life again—reincarnation, if we so choose, Summer's breeze shall never cease.

Original poem by Martha Woodruff-Duncan Copyright

Fall

The season of Fall is here, with all of its splendor so dear. Bright yellow leaves that turn gold, coral leaves that turn crimson, bright orange leaves that turn flaming red, purple, and maroon. It speaks to us in so many tones of joy, if we just stop to listen to its envoy. But we don't have much time because the splendor of Fall will soon have to be recalled, returning itself to the slumber of a season known to all—Winter!

Original poem by Martha Woodruff-Duncan Copyright

Winter

◇◇

Winter comes with such a bite, but much to everyone's delight. Snowflakes fall to cover all, leaving Earth a crystal ball. A Winter wonderland it is for all of us to love in bliss.

Original poem by Martha Woodruff-Duncan Copyright

CHRISTMAS

Christmas comes with such a song that lasts the whole day long. Snowflakes fall from up above so high like a wedding in the sky. Angels sing, sweet bells ring, all in celebration of Christ the King.

Original poem by Martha Woodruff-Duncan Copyright

Easter

◇◇◇

Easter comes with such great cheer, its message loud and clear for everyone to hear. A Christ arisen as we know, who beholds both friend and foe, teaching us to harbor no foe.

Original poem by Martha Woodruff-Duncan Copyright

Acceptance

When we live in acceptance of what is, we no longer find it necessary to resist, raise our fist to the heavens in retaliation, but face what is as we let it all fizz itself out without a shout.

What we resist, persists. What we fear, we create. This is a Universal Law. When we know this, we no longer shout and spout as we move all about, feel the clout in the darkness of fear that smears our consciousness with so much doubt.

We fail to learn as we turn in this direction, in that direction, and continue to slam into a brick wall where we fall and feel so small we cannot stand tall. We let our present situation devour our consciousness, disintegrate it into a whirlwind of fear and endless perpetuation of what we face with dismay.

Acceptance means letting it be, setting it free. Go about without any doubt that the resolve is there. There is no such thing as unfair, but wear the armor of life that we chose as we close the door of fear, crushing it with a spear—the spear of our awakened consciousness.

CONTINUATION...

No more to sleep so very deep, but come back home to who we really are—a manifesting fifth-dimensional consciousness who has traveled so very far. No more to fall because we know it all, and the Godhead, the Father of us all, our Creator, will be there to embrace our awakening as we stand in Its brilliant light, with all our might, as in the beginning—created in Its image and likeness—a manifesting fifth-dimensional consciousness.

Original poem by Martha Woodruff-Duncan Copyright

The Essence of God

We are all a part of the Godhead at all times, we are never separated from Its Divine Essence, we just think we are through our thoughts and our feelings, but in reality we are connected to the Godhead at all times. God gave us free will to do as we will until we get our fill, but we have to remember that it is only a play (as on a stage), none of it is real, just what we feel. The feelings are our treasure, this is what gives us pleasure.

How far we have fallen from grace and can't find our place, sunken into the third-dimensional consciousness we have created through our thoughts and our feelings, lifetime after lifetime, inhabiting a new physical form as we continue to sleep and weep so deep.

We have to wake up, but we can only do so by realizing who we really are—a manifesting fifth-dimensional consciousness as our Divine Father—created in Its image and likeness in the beginning. We have fallen from our Divine Intelligence. The Godhead of us all does not see us as shameful and disgraceful, but as brilliant lights, Its

CONTINUATION...

creation, who have allowed ourselves to fall into darkness by allowing ourselves to get tangled up in our illusory life cycle experiences on Planet Earth (our playground and stage), lifetime after lifetime, causing us to progress so very slow—spiritually—as we continue to view our woes. We view each life journey in our physical form as such a long time as we continue to stumble, fumble, and grumble through each lifetime, but in reality, it is only a blink of an eye in duration.

Given free will, we can only come back home on our own, out of darkness into the brilliant lights that we are, no more to spar with each other, but allow ourselves to be who we are—a manifesting fifth-dimensional consciousness.

Original poem by Martha Woodruff-Duncan Copyright

Reflections

It is good to reflect in each moment of now on how we have lived our life so far. Those who do not have forgot how far we can go by letting it flow—make amends, let us be friends, knowing that it all depends on us to shake the gust of dust away, no more to say this or that, but let us get fat on feelings.

We pretend to forgive, but continue to live in this whirlwind of thought where we fought and forgot who we are. It is all just a game, which we preordain in advance, as we continue to do our dance again and again.

We don't get it, so we forget it—let it continue on with the same old song—this whirlwind of thought, thinking that we've done nothing wrong. Self-righteous we are, keeping ourselves from going afar, especially now in these critical changes to take place on our Planet Earth. Its cleansing is near, but there is nothing to fear, if we reflect in each moment of now and vow to see, to be, to know who we are and not bar ourselves from going afar.

CONTINUATION...

Reflections are good, they allow us to shave off the wood that grows within us through thoughts of negativity, resistance of what is, creating a path to wander amiss, keeping us from living in bliss. No more to sleep, no more to weep, knowing that it all just is for a purpose.

Original poem by Martha Woodruff-Duncan Copyright

In Honor of Love

In memory of Andrew David Duncan, my husband

We met each other broken, our words were unspoken, but we continued to stay together, light as a feather, as we weathered each moment of now. We did what we could and knocked on wood as we opened each door in those moments of now. I feel full of gain and have no blame as I let our flame burn. The flame of life that we lit, and together we sit. There are no exceptions, there are no deceptions, there is just life as it is in each moment of now. I will not waver but live in favor of our love.

Original poem by Martha Woodruff-Duncan Copyright

Moms

◇◇

*In memory of Teresa Leon, my mother-in-law,
and Anna Marie Woodruff, my mother*

Moms are great. They never hate, they always are, just like a star.

We grow and play, we face dismay, but moms are always just a thought away.

Original poem by Martha Woodruff-Duncan Copyright

BUTTERFLIES

In memory of D. Tina Robinson and Dr. Patrick A. Robinson, DDS, longtime cherished friends and confidants

I watch a butterfly flying so high as it says, "Hi and bye."

They see my human species fight and spite, creating strife to pollute all life. What must they think as they sit and drink out of a pond in a lovely landscaped park, commercial garden, or the garden of a lovely home?

"Oh my, why are those humans acting so bad when they could be glad instead of mad? But mad they are, and because of that, they don't go afar, they just stay where they are."

Will they wake up, go afar, reach a star? "I don't know," says the butterfly as it flies by so high saying, "Hi and bye."

"No more strife to pollute all life," says the butterfly. "Feel glee, let it be, go free to see all that is—the birds, the bees, the whispering

CONTINUATION...

insects in Summer's breeze." All that we see when we let it be, when we set ourselves free?

"You most certainly do," says the butterfly as it flies by so high saying, "Hi and bye."

Original poem by Martha Woodruff-Duncan Copyright

Jesus of Nazareth

The man named Jesus, who came from Nazareth, came to us over two-thousand years ago on a special mission. That mission was—and is—to save us from not knowing and never experiencing who we really are. He demonstrated this by showing us what we can become. Indeed, what we are—if we will only accept it. Jesus did not come to save us from everlasting damnation. There is no such thing as we have conceived it. The only thing we encounter—if we continue to "cling" to a life journey on Planet Earth just experienced—is remorse, anger, blame—all of which cause suffering. We bring this "suffering," as we view it, upon ourselves by not letting go, by not putting it down. Instead, we sit and frown. Let it be, set it free like a bumblebee. See and feel the gain inside each blame. Let us move onward and upward to a higher level of consciousness filled to the brim with feelings—what it felt like. Feelings are the language of the soul, indeed! Most certainly.

CONTINUATION...

When we understand this, when we know this, we pay the highest tribute to the man named Jesus of that lifetime, who came to us willingly, knowingly, and freely to tell us who we really are. This was his only mission. He suffered his crucifixion for us because he was not going to recant the truth—telling us and demonstrating to us who we really are. Jesus said, "I and the Father are One, and ye are my brethren." He demonstrated this truth through his death and resurrection for everyone to witness.

Original poem by Martha Woodruff-Duncan Copyright

About the Author

Martha Woodruff-Duncan is a retired legal secretary of twenty-eight years. She was born in New Mexico. Her mother, of Mexican descent, now deceased, taught school for forty years—second, third and fourth grades, at different stages of her teaching career. The last ten Summers of her teaching career she taught Project Head Start. Her father, of British descent, now deceased, always worked as a mechanic, having his own business with his three other brothers.

She feels grateful to reside in one of the most beautiful states in the country, western Washington. Being a resident of Seattle since February 1992, meeting her late husband in June of that year, has brought her a wealth of experiences. Destiny has a way of finding itself, she is thoroughly convinced of this now.

Printed in the USA
CPSIA information can be obtained
at www.ICGtesting.com
JSHW012123281023
50964JS00002B/14

9 781639 036899